THIS WORKBOOK BELONGS TO:

....

TABLE OF CONTENTS

Preface • **5**

Introduction • **7**

CHAPTER 1. Creating Safety • **9**

CHAPTER 2. Impact of Perspective • **15**

CHAPTER 3. Understanding Brain Plasticity • **20**

CHAPTER 4. Adverse Childhood Experiences • **24**

CHAPTER 5. Recognizing Brain Regions • **27**

CHAPTER 6. Brainstem • **32**

CHAPTER 7. Midbrain • **35**

CHAPTER 8. Limbic System • **38**

CHAPTER 9. Cortex • **43**

CHAPTER 10. Responses to Threat • **46**

CHAPTER 11. State-Dependent Functioning • **53**

CHAPTER 12. Somatosensory Regulation • **59**

CHAPTER 13. Emotions and Sensations • **64**

CHAPTER 14. Relational Regulation • **70**

CHAPTER 15. Cortical Regulation • **74**

CHAPTER 16. Regulate, Relate, Reason • **81**

CHAPTER 17. Trauma, Neglect, and Healing • **87**

CHAPTER 18. Next Steps • **91**

Appendix • **96**

Notes • **105**

Heart Rate Charts • **108**

PREFACE

Welcome to your NeuroLogic® Workbook. Our hope is that this information will empower you to make the most of the amazing learning and healing potential of your brain.

Understanding the brain can help you better recognize and manage emotions, control responses to stress, increase learning, and improve relationships. In adolescence, your brain and body are being inundated with a range of hormones and a barrage of new emotions and sensations. The information you will be learning can help you better understand yourself and your impact on others. It can empower you to take control of your learning and to better regulate your emotions and impulses.

Our hope is that this workbook will help you maximize your potential. The information included and activities you will be asked to do have the power to positively change your brain. No matter what adversity you have encountered in life, by understanding the brain more fully and applying this knowledge, you can experience positive change, improved learning, emotional healing, and growth.

"Mindfulness IS NOTICING YOUR THOUGHTS, FEELINGS, AND PHYSICAL SENSATIONS IN THE PRESENT MOMENT WITHOUT JUDGMENT IN AS MANY MOMENTS OF YOUR LIFE AS POSSIBLE."[1]

GINA BIEGEL

INTRODUCTION

■**Breathing and Mindfulness Exercises** You will find breathing exercises located in the back of this workbook. Your heart and brain are intricately connected. A focus on breathing is a fantastic way to learn to control your heart rate. Deep breathing improves the flow of oxygen to your brain, improving your brain's ability to process information. You may find some breathing exercises work better for you than others. It is important to practice them to find what works best for you.

You will also find mindfulness exercises in the back of this workbook. These exercises can promote integration of all levels of your brain by creating new neural pathways. They can reduce stress, increase focus, and improve attention and memory.[2]

These exercises may feel uncomfortable at first. Don't give up. If you stick with them, you will find them tremendously helpful. These are important skills that, with practice, can be used anywhere and anytime to keep yourself calm, focused and thinking clearly.

■**Practicing Gratitude** Gratitude has powerful physiological effects on your brain and your body. When you think about things or people you truly appreciate and are thankful for, your body and brain become calmer, and your attitude becomes more positive. Research has shown that students who do daily exercises in gratitude, such as keeping a gratitude journal, are more optimistic, feel better about school and life as a whole and have fewer physical complaints.[3] For this reason, there will be questions throughout this workbook to help you focus and experience the effects of gratitude.

■**Heart Rate** Your brain and heart are connected. Your heart rate is an indication of what is going on in the lower levels of your brain. It will be helpful to track your heart rate before and after various activities. Understanding the impact of these activities on your heart rate can empower you with new ideas and choices for self-regulation and stress reduction. Use the chart in the back of your workbook to track your heart rate.

"HE WHO
breathes
DEEPEST
lives
MOST." [4]

ELIZABETH BARRETT BROWNING

■ C H A P T E R 1

CREATING SAFETY

Write down 3-5 rules or expectations that are important to you in order to feel comfortable and safe in this learning environment.

1.

2.

3.

4.

5.

In order for you to feel open to learn and try new things, it is important that you feel safe. Your brain needs a safe environment to do its best learning and to take new risks. Dr. Sandra Bloom in her book, Creating Sanctuary, talks about the need for four kinds of safety.[5]

■ PHYSICAL SAFETY–Knowing that your body will not be hurt by others or by yourself.

■ EMOTIONAL SAFETY–Being safe with your feelings and knowing how to take care of yourself when your feelings become uncomfortable.

■ SOCIAL SAFETY–Feeling safe and cared about within a group.

■ MORAL SAFETY–Knowing right from wrong and trusting the people around you know right from wrong.

What types of safety are most important to you right now?

Personal Safety Plans

A personal safety plan is a predetermined list of things you can do to make sure you stay emotionally or physically safe, especially if a topic, activity, or environment feels potentially threatening to you. You may want to have safety plans for different situations that you encounter in life.

Examples of things that might be in a safety plan:
- Sit in a part of the room where you feel safest.
- Sit next to someone with whom you feel safe.
- Ask to pass on an activity or discussion question.
- Ask to get a drink of water or go to the bathroom.
- Put your head down and/or close your eyes for a few minutes.
- Distract yourself by doodling, journaling, or tapping the back of your hand.
- Tell someone you trust that you are feeling unsafe.
- Picture a safe and peaceful place where you feel comfortable.
- Focus on your breathing, taking slow and deep breaths.
- Zone out for a few minutes.
- Repeat a positive statement to yourself. "I am safe". I am not in danger.
- Relax your body.
- Focus on a specific sound, sight, or smell to distract yourself.

What are some specific emotions that you struggle with?

What situations are most likely to stir up these emotions?

With these things in mind, write a safety plan focused on things you will be able to do when you feel unsafe or threatened.

MY PERSONAL SAFETY PLAN

While in class, I can do the following things if I feel emotionally unsafe or threatened:

1.

2.

3.

4.

5.

6.

In other situations, I can do the following things to stay safe:

1.

2.

3.

4.

5.

6.

One way of keeping yourself feeling safe is to have a clear picture in your imagination of a safe place you can go anytime you want. After spending a few minutes picturing yourself in this safe and calm place, draw or use words to describe the place in as much detail as possible. Use all of your senses. What does it look like? What is around you? What do you feel? What do you smell and hear?

What was this experience like for you?

List two things for which you are grateful.

"REFLECT UPON YOUR *present blessings,* OF WHICH EVERY MAN HAS PLENTY; NOT ON YOUR PAST MISFORTUNES, OF WHICH ALL MEN HAVE SOME."[6]

CHARLES DICKENS

▪ CHAPTER 2

IMPACT OF PERSPECTIVE

Survey • Circle one of the statements in each pair that you believe best reflects the way you think.

1. If I am not good at something, I probably never will be.

2. If I stick with something, I can get better at it.

1. If my first plan fails, I give up.

2. If my first plan fails, I can figure out another way to do it.

1. Making mistakes is embarrassing.

2. Making mistakes is a chance to learn how to do it better next time.

1. My beliefs about people and the world are accurate and will not change.

2. My beliefs about people and the world are flexible and change with experiences.

1. You can only get straight A's if you are naturally smart.

2. Anyone can get straight A's if they work hard enough.

1. If you are impulsive, you will always be that way.

2. You can change how impulsive you are.

Count up the number of 1's and 2's that you circled and record that below.

Number of 1's _____ (Growth-limiting perspective)

Number of 2's _____ (Growth-producing perspective)

15

The brain has an amazing capacity to change. Your brain is like a muscle. Change comes as a result of repetition. When a part of your brain is activated over and over, it changes.

> *"Failure is a part of life. It's a part of building character and growing. Without failure, who would you be? I wouldn't be here if I hadn't fallen thousands of times, made mistakes. If something's going on in your life and you're struggling, embrace it because you're growing."*[7]
> **Nick Foles** Philadelphia Eagles Quarterback after winning Super Bowl LII.

Do you agree with this quote? Why or why not?

> *"For thirty years, my research has shown that the view you adopt for yourself profoundly affects the way you lead your life. It can determine whether you become the person you want to be and whether you accomplish the things you value."*[8] **Carol S. Dweck**

Psychologist and researcher Carol Dweck found one important difference between people who were more successful and those who were not. The difference was the person's perspective or "mindset". Unsuccessful people believed you are either born smart or talented or not. Successful people, on the other hand, believed that growth was always possible. They understood that you can get smarter by working on it and that talent and skills get better with practice.[9]

Describe a time when your perspective helped you achieve something or was part of your lack of achievement.

What do you think it takes to have or keep a perspective that leads towards growth?

According to the survey, would you say you have more of a growth-limiting or growth-producing perspective?

Do you believe you can get better at the things you struggle with? Why or why not?

Does your perspective vary in regard to different areas of your life? If so, how?

To give yourself a visual picture of your approach to life, divide the circle below into a pie chart with different pieces representing different areas of your life (school, relationships, activities, etc). In each piece of the chart, give a visual representation of your perspective for that category by coloring or shading in the percentage that you feel you can grow or change in that area.

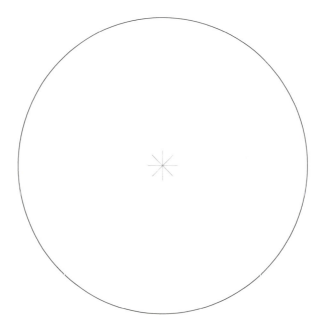

One area of my life that I can work on developing a more positive perspective towards growth is:

List two things for which you are grateful.

"Plasticity
IS THE PROCESS
THROUGH WHICH THE
OUTSIDE WORLD
GETS INSIDE US
AND CHANGES US.
IF EXPERIENCES
DID NOT ACTUALLY
CHANGE THE BRAIN,
WE WOULD NEVER
BE ABLE TO
REMEMBER
ANYTHING." [10]

LAURENCE STEINBERG

CHAPTER 3

UNDERSTANDING BRAIN PLASTICITY

Much of the following information is adapted from the Neurosequential Model of Therapeutics (NMT) and the Neurosequential Model of Education (NME) developed by the ChildTrauma Academy.[11]

List two or three things that have changed about your brain over the past month. This could be something you learned, a skill you developed, thought patterns or habits you changed, or relationship skills you developed.

The brain's ability to change is called plasticity. Our brains control everything we do. What we think, how we act, how we react, and what we hope and dream all trace back to our brain, and all can be changed.

Childhood

When you are born, your brain has already developed the 86 billion brain cells, called neurons, it will need throughout life. Experiences cause these neurons to connect with other neurons. Repeated experiences allow connections to become strong pathways, permanently etched into the brain. By the age of 8 months, an infant living in a safe and loving environment will have formed 500 trillion of these connections. By age two these connections have doubled. By the time a child is three years old, the brain structure and design which provides the foundation for future functioning is almost complete.

Adolescence

During the adolescent years, there is a period of intense brain rewiring and activity. Your brain is fine-tuning and zeroing in on what is most important as you prepare for adulthood. It is getting rid of neurons that are not being used and making the pathways for those that are being used faster and faster. It is important to make sure you are exercising all parts of your brain during this time and using all the connections that are important to you now and will be important in the future.

Since adolescence is a time when your brain will get smarter and quicker at the things that you do most often, what are some things you might want to consider doing more or less often?

Since your brain will lose neurons and connections that are not being used, list any skill, activity, or topic of learning that you have stopped working on, that you might consider resuming?

How to Change the Brain

In order to change or develop any specific area of your brain, that area or pathway needs to be activated in a patterned, repetitive manner. Your brain changes by doing a new thing over and over again. Repetition can solidify good or bad habits. Doing anything, including the wrong thing again and again, can make the action become automatic.

List two examples that show the plasticity of the brain.

Knowing that you can change your brain including habits, thought patterns, reactions, skills or knowledge, what is a change you may like to work towards?

What are some steps you could take towards implementing this brain change?

List two things for which you are grateful.

"PSYCHOLOGISTS SAY
THAT HAVING A
grandparent
WHO LOVES YOU, A
teacher
WHO UNDERSTANDS
AND BELIEVES IN YOU,
OR A TRUSTED
friend
YOU CAN CONFIDE IN
MAY MITIGATE
THE LONG-TERM
EFFECTS OF
EARLY TRAUMA."[12]

DANNY DE BELIUS

CHAPTER 4

ADVERSE CHILDHOOD EXPERIENCES

The Impact of Adverse Experiences

Research has shown that early adverse experiences can have a tremendous impact on your future and your health. There was a study done in the late 1990's called the Adverse Childhood Experiences Study (ACEs). Over 17,000 adults were asked ten questions which focused on common types of childhood abuse and neglect. The answers to these ten questions determined their ACE score. The study showed that the higher the number of adverse experiences, the greater the risk was for some significant health-related issues.[13]

People who have had adverse experiences are often more sensitive to stress and may, therefore, react more strongly to additional stress. If you have experienced some type of trauma or neglect, chances are that your brain has been impacted. This impact can play out differently for different people. Some results could be poor academic achievement, depression, lack of impulse control, health issues, alcoholism, and acting out behaviors.

For those that have been impacted by adverse experiences, it is important to recognize that you are not alone. You cannot change what happened to you, but you can make changes to lessen the impact of these experiences moving forward. There is well-documented research that shows how your brain and body can counteract the negative impact of adverse experiences through things you do and the relationships you have.[14] Close relationships are one of the keys to building resilience.

"There are people with high ACE scores who do remarkably well. Resilience builds throughout life and close relationships are key."[15] **Jack Shonkoff**

24

Name the people in your life that support you and give you hope.

In upcoming chapters, you will take a closer look at how to bring healing to the regions of the brain, which may be impacted by early childhood trauma or neglect. In the meantime, practice the breathing and mindfulness exercises you have been learning. This is a great first step towards promoting a healthy brain.

Take a moment to express your feelings through words or pictures regarding what you have learned so far.

Name the people in your life who love you, understand you and believe in you.

Who can you talk to about the things that you struggle with? Do you?

What is your level of hope for making positive changes on a scale of 0-10 with 10 being excellent? Why did you choose that number?

PRACTICING GRATITUDE

List two things for which you are grateful.

■ CHAPTER 5

RECOGNIZING BRAIN REGIONS

The information in chapters 5-11 is adapted from the Neurosequential Model of Therapeutics (NMT) and the Neurosequential Model of Education (NME) developed by the ChildTrauma Academy.[16]

Make your best guess on which part of the brain you think would be hardest to change. Label the following 1-4 with 1 being the hardest to change and 4 being most easily changeable.

_____ Part that controls heart, breathing, and temperature

_____ Part that controls muscle movement and fine motor skills

_____ Part that controls relationships and emotions

_____ Part that controls learning and taking in new information

The brain is much more complex than this picture, but this is a great tool to help you understand and remember how your brain functions. The brain develops from the bottom up. Different parts develop at different ages. Positive and negative experiences impact whatever area of the brain is developing at that time.

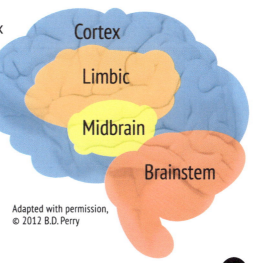

Adapted with permission, © 2012 B.D. Perry

Brainstem

The brainstem is the first part of the brain to develop. It develops first because it is needed to regulate our most basic survival needs. It is located at the bottom of the brain above the neck.

When does the brainstem develop?

What is the brainstem responsible for?

Midbrain

The midbrain is the second part of the brain to develop. It is connected to the brainstem. It is often called the reptilian brain because this is where the brains of reptiles stop growing.

When does the midbrain develop?

What is the midbrain responsible for?

Limbic System

The third part of the brain to develop is the limbic system. It is located in the middle of the brain.

When does the limbic system develop?

What is the limbic system responsible for?

Cortex

The cortex sits on the top of the brain and is the last part of the brain to fully develop.

When does the cortex develop?

What is the cortex responsible for?

All Parts of the Brain Work Together.

When traumatic events have impacted the lower regions of the brain, all areas are impacted. Information must filter through the bottom areas of the brain in order to get to the cortex. If the bottom areas are overdeveloped due to stress and/or if the cortex is underdeveloped, the ability of the cortex to control the impulses coming from these lower regions can be significantly impaired.

Why might it be important to understand the different regions of the brain?

List two things for which you are grateful.

"All parts of the brain can modify their functioning IN RESPONSE TO SPECIFIC, REPETITIVE PATTERNS OF ACTIVATION." [17]

BRUCE D. PERRY

CHAPTER 6

BRAINSTEM

Write down an example of a way your brain has changed in the past week.

The brainstem is responsible for life-sustaining functions such as regulating heart rate, temperature, breathing, and blood pressure. The brainstem also controls metabolism and the ability to pay attention. The brainstem develops almost completely while a baby is in utero. If something goes wrong during pregnancy, delivery, or the first few months of life, there may be some areas of the brainstem that are under or overdeveloped.

The brainstem is very sensitive to signals of fear, distress, and danger. Because it is reflexive, it reacts instantaneously in response to stress signals in the environment. It is the hardest part of the brain to change but can still be changed with time and effort.

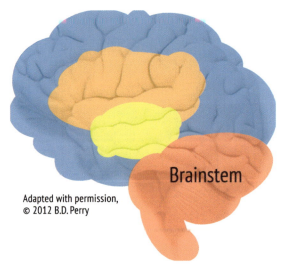

Adapted with permission,
© 2012 B.D. Perry

What are some signs that there may be issues with the development of the brainstem?

Many of the things you would use to calm a newborn infant are helpful in calming and developing the brainstem. Remember, to be able to change any part of the brain, patterned, repetitive activation is needed.

List some activities or interventions that can help calm and/or develop the brainstem.

What are some things that you learned about the brainstem?

List some things you can do to help calm or regulate your brainstem.

Which one or two of these things are you willing to try this week? (If you are able, record the impact each activity has on your heart rate.)

List two things for which you are grateful.

■ CHAPTER 7

MIDBRAIN

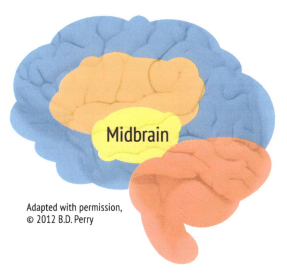

Adapted with permission,
© 2012 B.D. Perry

Remember that the midbrain is the second part of the brain to develop. The midbrain is reactive, not thinking or feeling. It is responsible for the following:

- Fine motor skills
- Large motor skills
- Movement and balance
- Appetite
- Salivation, swallowing
- Sleep
- Directing sense impulses throughout the body
- Maintaining equilibrium
- Sense of smell and taste
- Hearing

What are some signs that there may be issues with the development of the midbrain?

List some of the activities or interventions that can help calm and/or develop the midbrain.

      Whether the midbrain had problems in development or not, all of us can benefit from knowing, using, and understanding midbrain interventions. All information enters your brain through the brainstem and then goes up through your midbrain. Learning to calm your brain through the brainstem and midbrain can be instrumental to calming yourself down when upset. Remember that it is important for activities to be done in a patterned and repetitive manner throughout the day for the greatest effectiveness.

How do you currently use large and small muscle movement throughout the day? (For example, do you pace while talking, move your arms a lot, doodle, fidget, tap your fingers, play sports, rock, spin, bounce?)

Based on what you learned about large and small muscle movement and balance, make a list of some of the activities or interventions that may be helpful for you to work into your schedule or use throughout the day.

Name one or two things from this list that you are willing to try this week.

List two things for which you are grateful.

CHAPTER 8

LIMBIC SYSTEM

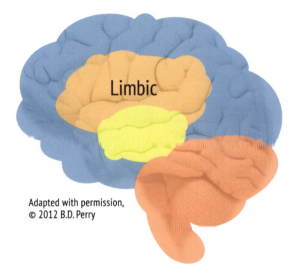

Adapted with permission, © 2012 B.D. Perry

The limbic system is located in the middle of the brain. It continues to develop through adolescence. The limbic system is responsible for:

- Relationships
- Emotional reactivity
- Short-term memory

What are some signs that there may be issues in the development of the limbic system?

Whether there are limbic system issues or not, all of us can benefit from knowing, using, and understanding ways to develop and calm our limbic systems. Learning to understand emotions and relationships in terms of what is going on in your brain can be instrumental in helping to learn, grow, build relationships, and make decisions.

What interventions can help to calm or develop the limbic system?

Your need for relationships is as innately wired as your need to eat, drink and sleep and is every bit as important. Positive, healthy relationships are important for your brain. We all learn, grow and regulate our actions better when we are around people who love and care about us.

What do you look for in a friend?

If you have unhealthy relationship patterns, you can work to change them. Each new positive relationship potentially sets a new template for positive healthy relationships. Changing relationship patterns will take time. Your brain pulls you towards what is familiar and the unfamiliar can feel unsafe and scary. If you have struggled with relationships, here are things that might help:

- Practice your relationship skills with safe, caring adults.
- Keep your list of positive qualities in mind when looking for friends.
- Work to be the kind of friend that fits that list.
- Look for healthy, trustworthy people.
- Take small risks to know someone.
- Focus on the positive.
- Talk with a counselor about past issues if you find yourself struggling with trust or attachment issues.

Who do you turn to when you need to talk?

What makes a person worthy of your trust?

What kind of relationship risks are you taking now?

What changes are needed to help you take more positive risks?

List two things for which you are grateful.

"IN ORDER TO KEEP THE BRAIN FIT, *we must learn something new,* RATHER THAN SIMPLY REPLAYING ALREADY-MASTERED SKILLS."[18]

NORMAN DOIDGE

CHAPTER 9

CORTEX

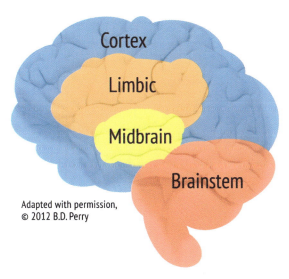
Adapted with permission, © 2012 B.D. Perry

The cortex continues to develop through adulthood. It is responsible for:
- Abstract thought
- Concrete thought
- Verbal and non-verbal communication
- Judgment
- Problem-solving ability
- Insight/self-awareness
- Self-image
- Reading and writing
- Ability to modulate and control behavior
- Mathematical reasoning

Since the cortex is still developing through adulthood, we all have the ability to continue to learn and get better in these areas. Every cortex is unique. It is possible for you to be right on track for your age group with a cortical skill or to be developmentally years ahead or years behind, depending on the experiences you have had or not had in life. This is why it is not helpful to compare yourself to others.

If you are behind others your age in your reading ability, for instance, you are not "a bad reader." You just need more time and experience reading. Remember that neural connections are made by repetition. If you exercise your "reading muscle," it will grow. The same can be true for any other skills.

List some signs of an underdeveloped cortex.

Whether areas of your cortex are underdeveloped or not, all of us can benefit from strengthening the cortex. As you develop your cortex, you are strengthening your reasoning, impulse control, insight, creativity, and decision making. Your cortex is what allows you to learn new things, think about what you are doing, make plans for the future, be creative, and solve difficult problems.

What types of things can help to develop the cortex?

Two important aspects of strengthening the cortex are repetition and novelty. If you practice the same thing over and over, that skill will get better and faster. When you try something new, your brain will actually form new neurons and new neural connections. Both of these are important for the growth and development of the cortex.

What activities do you currently participate in during the week that are developing your cortex?

Based on what you learned about the cortex, list some things that may be helpful to start doing or spend more time doing.

List two things for which you are grateful.

■ CHAPTER 10

RESPONSES TO THREAT

Your brain is always on the lookout for threat and danger. It assesses information coming from both the external and internal world and reacts instantaneously to assess the information and initiate the response that will keep you safe. A threat can be anything that makes you feel uncomfortable.

Give some examples of different things that may trigger the threat response

Internal

External

Sometimes your brain's reaction to threat can be set off by something that is not an actual threat. A person may be in a safe environment and the brain can still respond as if the environment is dangerous. This reaction can be triggered by past experiences and conscious or unconscious memories. A trigger can be a certain smell, a sound, a touch, a familiar face or anything that reminds you of the traumatic experience you have gone through before.

When you feel threatened, a complex, total body response begins which is directed and controlled by your brain. Your brain shifts along a continuum of internal states to make sure you stay safe and have the resources you need to combat the threat. There are five internal states that function as a continuum. The five states are calm, alert, alarm, fear and terror.

The following chart indicates which part of your brain is most in control during various states along this continuum. This is important because each region of your brain manages and processes information in a very different way.

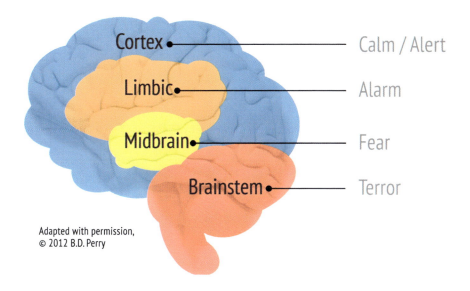

Adapted with permission,
© 2012 B.D. Perry

These internal states affect everything you do, including the way you think, act and feel.

Write what you have learned about each state.

Calm

Alert

Alarm

Fear

Terror

Note: Fear and Terror may be experienced as anger and rage.

Heart Rate

These internal states impact your heart rate. If your brain is preparing you to fight or flee, your heart rate goes up as you move down through these states. If your brain is preparing you to dissociate (zone out and shut down), your heart rate will decrease.

How can this information be helpful?

Adaptive Responses to Threat

Different people have different learned ways of responding as they feel threatened and move through this continuum of states. What feels threatening may be different for each individual, as well as which style of response they might use. There are two very different responses that people primarily follow when they feel threatened. Some people use a "fight or flight" response. Others use a "giving up or surrendering" response. Many use a combination of both of these responses.

Describe the "fight or flight" response.

Describe the "giving up or surrendering" also called the dissociative response.

What would be a mixed response?

REFLECTION

How would you describe your most often used response when you feel threatened?

When and how often do you find yourself in a state of calm?

What helps calm you down when you are in a state of alarm or fear?

How can understanding the threat response be helpful to you?

List two things for which you are grateful.

"In between every action and reaction, THERE IS A SPACE. USUALLY, THE SPACE IS EXTREMELY SMALL BECAUSE WE REACT SO QUICKLY, BUT TAKE NOTICE OF THAT SPACE AND EXPAND IT. BE AWARE IN THAT SPACE THAT you have a choice to make."[19]

REBECCA EANES

CHAPTER 11

STATE-DEPENDENT FUNCTIONING

State-Dependent Thinking

When you shift in the continuum of states and move from one region of the brain being in control to another, your style of thinking changes as well as your functional intelligence.

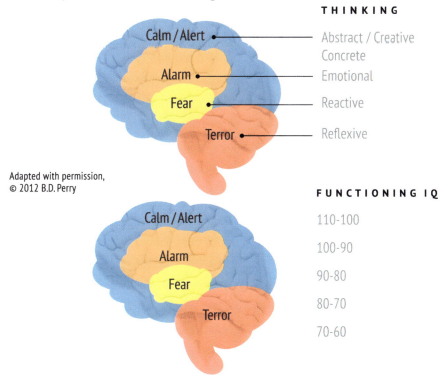

Adapted with permission, © 2012 B.D. Perry

When your brain is calm, you can think abstractly and creatively using the smartest part of your cortex. When you are in an alert state, you are using the lower, concrete thinking part of your cortex. In an alarm state, your brain shifts to the limbic system and your thinking becomes emotional. In a state of fear, you are no longer thinking but basically reacting from the midbrain. In a state of terror, your actions become completely reflexive coming from the brainstem.

Describe how each of the following states impacts your thinking and functional intelligence.

Calm

Alert

Alarm

Fear

Terror

Your state also impacts how you experience time.

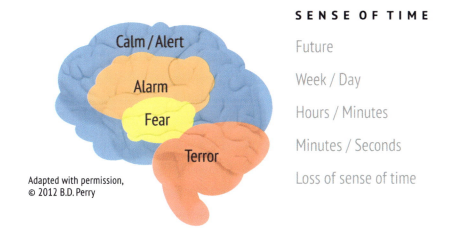

SENSE OF TIME

Future

Week / Day

Hours / Minutes

Minutes / Seconds

Loss of sense of time

Adapted with permission, © 2012 B.D. Perry

Describe a time when you were in one of these states and your sense of time matched this chart.

It can be very difficult to counteract a state-dependent shift in the moment. If you notice it happening while you still have access to your cortex, you can make decisions and choose strategies that help you move to a calmer state. In these instances, your safety plan can be very helpful.

Your safety plan is like your fire drill. It needs to be practiced when you are not under threat and shared with those who can help and direct you if you find yourself in a state of alarm, fear or terror. Consider adding to your safety plan those things you would want others to know in order to help you if you are in a state where you are unable to think clearly for yourself.

What are your personal warning signs or triggers for shifting into a state of alarm or fear?

What are some possible physical clues that you are in a state of alarm or fear?

REFLECTION

How does what you learned in this chapter help you to understand yourself and/or others better?

What are two strategies that you could use when you notice yourself getting anxious or upset that could help you return to a calmer state?

Name some people in your life who may be able to help you calm down if they were aware of the strategies in your safety plan.

Who from this list are you willing to share these strategies with this week?

PRACTICING GRATITUDE
List two things for which you are grateful.

"*Regulation*
GIVES US THE ABILITY
TO PUT TIME AND THOUGHT
BETWEEN A FEELING
AND AN ACTION."[20]

BRUCE D. PERRY

■ CHAPTER 12

SOMATOSENSORY REGULATION

If you catch yourself beginning to feel agitated, frustrated, anxious or upset, it is helpful to have strategies that assist you in moving towards a calmer state. A term for this is regulation.

Using your senses and movement is a great way to stay regulated and keep yourself in a calm or alert state. All information enters the brainstem through one of your senses. Understanding your senses and sensory preferences is key to learning how to regulate your emotions, thoughts, and behaviors and increase your ability to learn. We can use our senses to calm ourselves down and to wake ourselves up.

What are some things you do or see others doing to wake themselves up?

What are some things you do or see others doing to calm themselves down?

Taste • Foods that have crunchy textures or cold temperatures are usually alerting. Foods that are sweet or warm are usually good for calming.

List some things you can eat, drink or chew on to stay awake and alert.

List some things you can eat, drink or chew on when you want to calm down.

Touch • In general, a cold environment or a light, unexpected or rough touch is often alerting. A warm environment or a predictable, patterned touch with some pressure is often calming.

What are some school-appropriate ways you could use your sense of touch to keep yourself energized or to calm yourself down?

Visual • For the most part dim lighting, muted shades of blue and green, dark colors, and predictable patterns can be calming.

What visual environment do you find most calming?

List some things you can look at to calm yourself down and bring a sense of comfort or joy.

Smell • In general, familiar smells that are associated with familiar comforting experiences, interactions, or people are calming.

What smells are calming for you?

What smells are energizing?

Sound • Sounds that are calming and easiest for the nervous system to ignore are ones that are familiar, quiet, patterned, rhythmic and repetitive. Music that has the same rhythm as a mother's heartbeat has been found to be most calming.

What music or sounds help to energize you?

What music or sounds tend to calm you down?

Movement • Slow rocking, linear motions and repetitive, rhythmic movements have a calming effect on the nervous system. Movements that are fast-paced, jerky, abrupt or change direction quickly can be alerting.

What types of movement are calming for you?

What types of movement are good for energizing you?

In summary, write, draw or doodle what you have learned about your senses.

Things I can do to calm down

Things I can do to increase energy or alertness

Name two things you can use in school if you need to calm down and two things you can use if you need to become more alert.

List two things for which you are grateful.

CHAPTER 13

EMOTIONS AND SENSATIONS

The degree to which you can understand and manage painful or disorienting sensations may directly impact your ability to regulate emotions and behaviors. Recognizing sensations before emotional intensity increases can be instrumental in choosing regulation strategies before dysregulation occurs.

List or draw the sensations you feel with each of the following emotions:

Happy   Sad

Angry **Afraid**

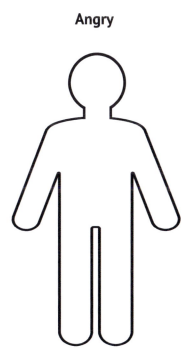 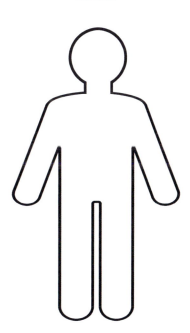

Your emotions can be experienced on a continuum from high to low intensity. When mindful of your sensations as they connect to your emotions, you can be better able to notice emotions before the intensity gets too uncomfortable. Recognizing emotions at lower intensity levels will allow you more time and more choices to regulate, focus and feel better.

List varying intensities of the following emotions.

Happy

Sad

Angry

Afraid

Comfortable

REFLECTION

Pick three emotion words from your lists above and give examples of when you might feel this way (I.e. I feel grumpy when ; I feel frustrated when...; I feel furious when...).

1.

2.

3.

Fill in a large heart with your current emotions. Give each emotion a percentage exemplifying how much time and space it takes up in your life. Color in each emotion with varying intensity of colors to represent the varying intensities you are experiencing.

What are some calming strategies you have learned that could help to calm you when experiencing uncomfortable intensities of emotions?

List two things for which you are grateful.

"FIRE CAN WARM OR CONSUME,
WATER CAN QUENCH OR DROWN,
WIND CAN CARESS OR CUT.
*And so it is with
human relationships:*
WE CAN BOTH CREATE AND DESTROY,
NURTURE AND TERRORIZE,
TRAUMATIZE AND HEAL EACH OTHER." [21]

BRUCE D. PERRY

CHAPTER 14

RELATIONAL REGULATION

As you become uncomfortable in a situation and move towards a state of alarm, your limbic system begins to take control. Once your limbic system takes over, your cortex is no longer in control and your thinking and decision making becomes emotional. If those around you are calm, safe and caring, they may be able to help you push through the uncomfortable feelings and return to a calmer state. This is called relational regulation.

Mirror Neurons

Mirror Neurons are a special class of brain cells that fire not only when you perform an action, but also when you observe someone else performing the action. These neurons appear to allow us not only to understand another person's actions but actually to feel what they are feeling. This is why it is so crucial that you choose your relationships and who you hang around with carefully. Emotions are contagious. You will be impacted by those you associate with because of mirror neurons.

What do you think the quote on page 69 means?

Your relationship templates or patterns were established during your early years of life. As a baby, your brain made connections regarding what to expect from people, based on those who first took care of you. If your needs were met, your brain decided that people were to be trusted. If your needs went unmet, or those who were supposed to care for you hurt you, your brain decided people were not to be trusted. If those caring for you were inconsistent, your brain decided that people were unpredictable. Whatever patterns were established became deeply ingrained as your brain formed its first neural connections and pathways regarding these first relationships in life.

As time went on, you experienced many other relationships, both good and bad. With each new relationship and interaction, your brain had to decide whether this relationship fit with the strong neural pathway already formed or whether this was different and needed a new neural pathway. It is easier to place people on an already existing pathway than to form a new pathway. It takes more effort and repetition to form new pathways.

It is important to have people in your life who care about and support you. You will do your best learning and decision making when you are cared for and feel safe. You can take more risks at learning new information, developing new skills and/or changing behaviors when you are in the presence of those who care about and support you.

How do you think the neural pathways your brain created during the first few years of life impact your relationships now?

How would you describe your approach to relationships now?

What kind of relationship risks are you taking now? Are these positive risks? Why or why not?

Who do you turn to when you need to talk? What impact does this person have on your emotions and your ability to move towards a state of calm?

PRACTICING GRATITUDE

List two things for which you are grateful.

"*Relational connectedness* BUFFERS CURRENT DISTRESS AND HELPS HEAL PAST TRAUMA."[22]

BRUCE D. PERRY

CHAPTER 15

CORTICAL REGULATION

When the lower regions of your brain are regulated, you have the best access to the smartest part of your brain, your cortex. Your cortex is what allows you to learn, think, be creative and solve problems. A strong, healthy cortex is able to intervene and help you control your impulses through reasoning, reflection, and problem-solving. When your cortex is able to help you control the lower regions of your brain, this is called cortical regulation

Cortical regulation involves using the cognitive skills of reasoning, critical thinking, self-monitoring, problem-solving, planning and insight. If you are lacking in knowledge regarding a particular problem, you can pursue information and gain the knowledge you need. You are able to converse with positive, healthy people in your life to get perspective on your thoughts and patterns. If your thoughts and self-talk are negative, you are able to change them and rethink your approach to a problem. Counseling with a professional can also be a big help if you find yourself stuck in unhealthy behaviors or thought patterns.

Gratitude

Gratitude is one example of cortical regulation. It is a way of thinking that allows you to change your focus. It has been shown to have a significant impact on a person's health and wellbeing. When you are able to access your cortex, you can choose to focus on what is good and positive in your life and be thankful for it rather than choosing to focus on the negative. Your choice of focus will impact your attitude, emotions, and well-being.

"Reflect upon your present blessings, of which every man has plenty; not on your past misfortunes, of which all men have some." **Charles Dickens**

List 5-10 things for which you are grateful.

Empathy

It's easy to assume that others see things the same way we do, but this is not always true. Your cortex has the ability to allow you to put yourself mentally in another person's place so that you can understand what they are feeling or experiencing. This is called empathy.

Name some things you can do to learn and build empathy regarding other people's feelings and viewpoints.

Self-Talk/Affirmation
Change each statement into a positive response to the same situation.

1. **You fail a test.**
   - Negative statement to self: I am stupid.
   - Changed statement:

2. **You trip and drop your books in the hallway.**
   - Negative statement: I am such a klutz.
   - Changed statement:

3. **Your boyfriend or girlfriend breaks up with you.**
   - Negative statement: I am such a loser; no one will ever love me.
   - Changed statement:

4. **You get anxious and can't remember the information you studied for a test.**
   - Negative statement: Why bother studying? My brain never works the way it should.
   - Changed statement:

5. **You have a fight with a friend and you both say mean things that you truly regret.**
   - Negative statement: Why do I pick such horrible friends? No one really cares.
   - Changed statement:

6. **A teacher has to redirect you for talking too much in class.**
   - Negative statement: This teacher hates me. Why bother trying to please her?
   - Changed statement:

7. **You feel depressed.**
   - Negative statement: Something is wrong with me. I am never going to be happy.
   - Changed statement:

8. **You try out for the basketball team but don't make it.**
   - Negative statement: I am just not good enough to play sports. I give up.
   - Changed statement:

9. **You are irritated by comments classmates are making.**
   - Negative statement: I can't handle these people. I'm walking out of class.
   - Changed statement:

10. **You are unhappy with your appearance.**
    - Negative statement: You are too ugly, fat, skinny, tall, short, or whatever you feel.
    - Changed statement:

How can you apply this information?

List some cortical regulation strategies that you use.

What are some additional cortical regulation strategies you would like to try or work to improve?

List two things for which you are grateful.

"ONCE YOU UNDERSTAND HOW *your body and brain* ARE PRIMED TO REACT IN CERTAIN SITUATIONS, YOU CAN START TO BE PROACTIVE ABOUT THINGS. YOU CAN IDENTIFY TRIGGERS AND KNOW HOW TO SUPPORT YOURSELF AND THOSE YOU LOVE."[23]

NADINE BURKE HARRIS

CHAPTER 16

REGULATE, RELATE, REASON

Dr. Bruce Perry uses the terms Regulate, Relate, Reason to help us remember the importance of approaching regulation from the bottom of the brain up.[24]

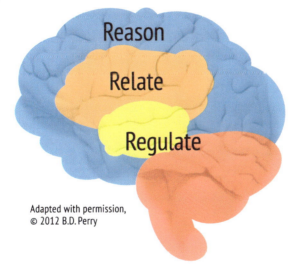

Adapted with permission,
© 2012 B.D. Perry

Regulate, Relate, Reason is a mantra that has great practical applications. It can be a helpful reminder to practice ongoing interventions throughout the day to maintain regulation starting with the bottom of your brain and working your way up. It can also be very helpful when dealing with others who are dysregulated. It gives you a roadmap or sequence of steps to follow.

"Regulate" is the first part of the sequence and refers to the physical calming strategies needed for the brainstem and midbrain. "Relate" is second and refers to the limbic or relational strategies that help you remain calm. "Reason" is the last part of the sequence and refers to the cognitive or cortical strategies you can use to help control and regulate all regions of your brain when your cortex is in control.

Triggers/Calming Skills

"Once you understand how your body and brain are primed to react in certain situations, you can start to be proactive about things. You can identify triggers and know how to support yourself and those you love." **Nadine Burke Harris**

Make a personal list of things that can trigger you to move to a state of alarm or fear.

If in a state of alarm or fear, the physical sensations that I may feel are:

Name some things you have learned that help calm you down.

Name some people with whom you can share your triggers and what works to calm you.

REGULATE, RELATE, REASON SAFETY PLAN

List things you have learned in previous chapters that can help you calm down using each level of the brain. Remember the importance of focusing your efforts from the bottom of the brain up.

Regulate

Relate

Reason

"In between every action and reaction, there is a space. Usually, the space is extremely small because we react so quickly, but take notice of that space and expand it. Be aware in that space that you have a choice to make." **Rebecca Eanes**

Do you believe any of the things you have learned could help you expand the space between an action and your reaction? Why or why not?

How will you use the mantra "regulate, relate, reason" to help yourself when upset?

How can you use this mantra to help others who are upset?

PRACTICING GRATITUDE
List two things for which you are grateful.

"TRAUMA REALLY DOES CONFRONT YOU WITH

the best and the worst.

YOU SEE THE HORRENDOUS THINGS THAT PEOPLE DO TO EACH OTHER, BUT YOU ALSO SEE RESILIENCY, THE POWER OF LOVE, THE POWER OF CARING, THE POWER OF COMMITMENT, THE POWER OF COMMITMENT TO ONESELF, THE KNOWLEDGE THAT THERE ARE THINGS THAT ARE LARGER THAN OUR INDIVIDUAL SURVIVAL."[25]

BESSEL VAN DER KOLK

CHAPTER 17

TRAUMA, NEGLECT, & HEALING

Trauma

"An experience is traumatic when it is overwhelming and uncontrollable and impacts victims by creating in them feelings of helplessness, vulnerability, loss of safety and loss of control."[26]

Not all fear-producing experiences create the same response in people. It is the response that determines whether the experience was traumatic, not the actual experience. Every child is unique, and a combination of personality, temperament, observations, experiences, and support network contribute to how he/she processes a traumatic event. Another factor is how quickly comfort and safety are reestablished. The more quickly there is intervention, the more likely that the event will have less long-standing traumatic results.

List some ways childhood trauma and/or neglect can impact a child.

> *"Relational connectedness buffers current distress and helps heal past trauma."*
>
> **Bruce D. Perry**

What do you think this means?

If you or someone you know has or is currently experiencing trauma, here are some steps to recovery.[27]

1. Make sure that you are safe. Recovery cannot start if the trauma is still ongoing in your life. If you are not safe, share this information with a trusted adult in your life.

2. Many times trauma can shatter self-esteem and self-worth. It is important to allow yourself to mourn what is lost.

3. Believe that you are capable and lovable to others.

4. Reestablish relationships with people who will have a positive impact on your life—relationships that promote safety, creativity, and joy.

5. Seek professional counseling. Trauma doesn't go away on its own. Talking about it with a professional can be a big help.

"Trauma really does confront you with the best and the worst. You see the horrendous things that people do to each other, but you also see resiliency, the power of love, the power of caring, the power of commitment, the power of commitment to oneself, the knowledge that there are things that are larger than our individual survival." **Bessel Van der Kolk**

What do you think this means?

What are the things you believe are most important in order to heal from trauma?

What are one or two things that you learned from this lesson?

How can you use this information to help others or help yourself?

List two things for which you are grateful.

CHAPTER 18

NEXT STEPS

You have learned that the impact early childhood adversity has on brain development can be very powerful and detrimental. Talking about trauma can bring up some strong feelings, particularly if you have experienced trauma to some degree in your own life. The good news is that much can be done to help the brain recover and heal. This restoration, which means that the brain is rewired to a better condition, is possible. You have been equipped with many things throughout these lessons to help develop and strengthen your brain.

Topics covered
1. Creating safety plans
2. The power of perspective
3. Brain plasticity
4. The impact of adverse experiences
5. The capacity to counteract the impact of adverse experiences by developing each region of your brain
6. Recognizing the roles of each brain region and what helps regulate them
7. Your brain's natural responses to threat
8. The impact of state-dependent functioning
9. Using your senses and movement to regulate the lower regions of your brain
10. The importance of relationships and impact of mirror neurons
11. The connection of sensations and emotions
12. The power of your thoughts and reasoning for regulation
13. The sequence of engagement: regulate, relate, reason
14. Breathing exercises
15. Mindfulness exercises
16. Gratitude expression

As you review this list of topics and activities, what stands out to you regarding ways you can strengthen and develop your brain?

Think about the interventions you have learned. Which have worked well in helping you to experience a greater sense of calm, a lower heart rate, and/or greater self-regulation?

Fill out a final version of the regulate, relate, reason safety plan to use when you feel yourself moving to a lower brain state.

MY REGULATE, RELATE, REASON SAFETY PLAN

Directions: Update your safety plan adding interventions from a regulate, relate, reason perspective.

While in school, I can do the following things to keep myself emotionally and mentally safe and calm:

◼ REGULATE

1.
2.
3.
4.
5.

◼ RELATE

1.
2.
3.
4.
5.

◼ REASON

1.
2.
3.
4.
5.

As you make positive choices to change the course of your life, others will be impacted by this change. Imagine yourself having made the changes you would like to make. You could think in terms of this month, year or multiple years. Picture what it looks like. You are doing well. You are successful. Think about where you are and what you are doing. Who is around you and how has your ripple effect impacted them? Add as much detail as possible to this vision and represent it below through words and images.

- **Draw your ripple effect.**

- As you make positive choices to change the course of your life, who else would be impacted by this change?

- If you keep applying the information and skills you have learned, what will be different for you in the future?

PRACTICING GRATITUDE
List two things for which you are grateful.

APPENDIX

BREATHING EXERCISES:

Breathing is a very powerful tool that can help you control your thoughts, feelings, behavior, and physiology. Slowing down your breathing helps slow down your heart rate. Slow, deep breathing increases the amount of oxygen that goes to your muscles, releasing tension. Focusing on breathing can slow down your thoughts and lower your anxiety level.

As you attempt to focus on your breathing, recognize that it may take some practice. It may actually raise your heart rate as it is a new experience that can make you self-conscious or anxious. Remember that you are in control of this process. You can stop whenever you want. You can choose to close your eyes or keep them open, focusing on a point on the wall or floor. It is important to practice deep breathing in a place where you feel relatively safe and comfortable. You may feel silly or uncomfortable the first few times but keep at it. With practice, you will find that you are able to use this skill easily in many different situations. Practicing these activities on your own in a safe, quiet place will increase your comfort level with them.

| SQUARE BREATHING | Adapted from Doodles, Dances and Ditties.[28]

Using a visual with breathing helps to add rhythm and pattern. For square breathing, you breathe in for a count of four, hold for a count of four, breathe out for a count of four, hold for a count of four, and then repeat. If you would like to add hand movements, you can trace a square in the air with one hand or trace a square on a desk or piece of paper. Check your heart rate and record it before and after the exercise.

| BELLY BREATHING | Adapted from The Mindfulness Toolbox by Donald Altman.[29]

Sit up straight in your chair and breathe normally. Keep breathing, but place one hand on your chest and one on your belly. Which hand is moving more? Is the air you are breathing traveling down to your belly, or is it stopping in your chest? Now reach your hands as far behind your back as you can without straining and keep breathing. Do you feel any difference in where the air you are breathing is going? Hold your arms back for 60 seconds and keep breathing.

| ENERGY BREATHING | Adapted from Doodles, Dances and Ditties.[30]

Take a long breath in while rubbing your hands together vigorously to a count of six. Then breathe out, while tapping the tips of your fingers together. Count slowly as you do this to a count of six in and six out. Repeat this for a minute or two.

| SIX-SECOND BREATHING | Adapted from Doodles, Dances and Ditties[31]

Stand with your arms at your sides. Breathe in as you slowly lift your arms out to the side and above your head (like wings) to a count of six. Then slowly lower your arms down to your sides at a count of six. Repeat this exercise for two to four minutes. This exercise is good for relaxing or for increasing energy.

| FIGURE EIGHT BREATHING | Adapted from the Brain Gym® movement, Lazy 8s.[32]

Hold a thumb up about 10–12 inches centered in front of your face. Using this as the center point, draw a sideways figure eight in front of your face with your thumb. Don't move your head but follow your thumb with your eyes. The movement should be slow and controlled, and the figure eight should be 12 to 16 inches wide. Once you have done this a couple of times, focus on breathing in as you cross the middle, and then breathe out as you cross the middle again. Repeat this 10–12 times.

| MINDFUL BREATHING COUNT |

Your breath can ground you to the present when your thoughts or emotions are taking you places you don't want to go. Notice your breath right now. Where is it entering your body? Is it coming in through your mouth or nose? Does it leave your body through your mouth or nose? Continue to take deep, slow breaths. Where is the air going inside your body? Is your belly rising as you breathe in and gently falling as you breathe out? Continue focusing on your breath and count as you breathe. Say to yourself, "Breathe in one," "breathe out one," "breathe in two," "breathe out two." Continue to count your breaths until you get to ten.

| RELAXING BREATH |

- Exhale completely through your mouth, making a whoosh sound to a count of six.
- Close your mouth and inhale quietly through your nose to a count of four.
- Hold your breath for a count of two.
- Exhale completely through your mouth again with a whoosh sound to a count of six.
- This is one breath. Now inhale again and repeat the cycle three more times for a total of four breaths.

Note the six, four, two count. If you have trouble holding your breath, you can speed up, but keep the ratio at 6:4:2, always exhaling longer than you inhale. This relaxing breath is a useful tool to use when something upsets you, to calm yourself down.

| HOOK UPS WITH EIGHT COUNT BREATHS | Adapted from the Brain Gym® movement, Hook ups.[33]

While sitting up straight or standing, cross your legs, extend your arms out in front of you with your hands back to back and thumbs pointing down. Put one arm over the other and interlock your fingers. Then bend your elbows, bringing your interlocked fingers down and then up to your chest. Hold this position. As you inhale, place your tongue flat against the roof of your mouth, about one-quarter of an inch behind your front teeth. Relax your tongue as you exhale. Rest in this posture while breathing in for a count of eight and breathing out for a count of eight. Repeat this for six to eight complete breaths.

MINDFULNESS EXERCISES

| SAFE PLACE |

Block out distractions for a couple of minutes by closing your eyes, putting your head down or focusing on a spot on your desk or a wall. Imagine a place where you can feel safe and calm. It can be anywhere you have ever been or a place you want to go. If you can't think of a place like this, imagine a place that you have seen on TV, or a place that you make up in your mind. Picture yourself in this place. Add as much detail as possible using all of your senses. What is around you? What do you see? What do you hear? What do you smell? What do you feel? Are you sitting, standing, laying down, or walking? Is there anyone there with you? Continue to imagine this in as much detail as possible. Once you have clearly established this place in your imagination, you can take yourself there as often as you need to when feeling stressed.

| MINDFUL EATING |

This exercise is to help you be more mindful – aware of your experiences and how your body is feeling at a given moment. We often eat candy without even thinking about it or fully enjoying the experience. If your mind wanders, don't allow yourself to get frustrated. Everyone's mind wanders. Don't judge yourself. This is something that takes practice. When you notice your mind wandering, just gently bring it back to the taste of the candy in your mouth. The more you are aware and pay attention to what your mind is doing the more you can control.

Take a piece of candy. Feel the weight and texture in your hand. Smell the candy, what is your body's reaction to the smell? Can you feel an increase of saliva? Put the candy in your mouth. What is the flavor? Let it roll around on your tongue. What does it taste like? Is it a strong taste? Pay attention to your mouth and continue to focus on the candy. What is its texture—is it smooth or rough? Can you taste it in different parts of your mouth? Be aware of how it feels on your tongue as it rolls around in your mouth. Be aware of this experience—is the candy enjoyable to eat? Is it getting smaller? What is happening to the texture? Continue to be aware of all your senses in relation to the candy and sit quietly being mindful for a little while longer.

| LEAVES FLOATING ON A STREAM |

The following exercise is an adaptation of a classic. The main purpose is to sit back and observe thoughts, emotions, and sensations rather than to get caught up in them. These things come and go like leaves floating down a stream. You don't need to react to them, just notice them.

Imagine yourself sitting next to a stream. You can close your eyes if you are comfortable or focus on a spot on the floor. Imagine each sense. What does the stream look like? What do you smell? What do you hear? Can you feel anything? The spray of water? A cool breeze? Bring your attention to your breath. Focus on breathing in and out. What is the temperature of the air you are breathing in? Does it change as it goes through your body? Continue to breathe in and out. With each breath out, imagine any tension leaving your body. Notice your muscles one at a time from your feet to your head and relax them as you breathe out.

Now begin to notice any emotions you may be feeling or thoughts you are thinking. Some emotions or thoughts may rush by and some may linger. Simply allow yourself to notice them. As you begin to notice thoughts or emotions, imagine putting them each on a leaf and letting them float by. Just let the thoughts and emotions come and watch them drift by. If any thoughts or emotions linger, keep focusing on the water flowing by. Your attention may wander. Painful thoughts or emotions may surface. You may begin to feel uncomfortable or think this exercise is "stupid." You may get stuck replaying a thought. That's okay. It is what our minds do. Continue to gently bring your focus back to your thoughts and emotions and place them on a leaf that is floating by. After a few minutes, bring your attention back to your breath. Focus on your breathing for a moment. When you are ready, open your eyes or look up.

| GRATITUDE |

It is easy at times to focus on the things that aren't going well or on the things we wish were different in our lives. What you focus on has a tremendous impact on your thinking, your emotions, and even your behavior. Gratitude has powerful physiological effects on your brain and your body. When you think about things or people you truly appreciate, your body and brain become calmer.

Make a list of things for which you are grateful. If you are struggling to come up with things, consider something you have in your life from the list below, picture life without it for a brief second, and then take time to appreciate and be grateful for its presence in your life.

- Sunshine
- Home
- Clothes
- Electricity
- Indoor Plumbing
- Friendships
- Technology
- Clean water to drink
- Animals
- Nature
- Adults who care
- Ability to speak and understand
- Transportation
- Family
- Health
- Seasons
- Your five senses
- Food
- Entertainment

| ACCORDION BREATHING |

You have a built-in nerve whose purpose is to regulate and relax you. This is called the vagus nerve. This nerve travels down your spine and links your brain with your heart and gut. There is a simple ancient practice that activates the vagus nerve in order to relax the brain and body and protect you from stress. You can do this exercise sitting or standing.

Bring your hands together in front of you with your palms touching. Notice the warmth between your palms and take a moment or two to focus on that. Now inhale and fill your belly with air as you move both arms outward like you are playing an accordion. When your arms are spread outward, hold your breath for a count of two. Then exhale slowly while bringing your arms inward and your palms back together for a count of four. Let all of the air out and allow your stress to flow out with each breath. Repeat this five times.

FOCUSING ON SENSES

Pay attention to your senses one at a time. First, focus on your sense of sight. Look around you. What do you see? Start with yourself. What do you notice about yourself, the position of your body, your clothes? Do you notice what is in front of you? What is behind you? What is to your right or to your left? What do you see as you look around the room? Now move to your sense of smell. Do you smell anything? Notice the air move in and out through your nose. Take a moment to notice any scents that come with that air. Now move to your sense of hearing. What can you hear right now? What noises surround you? Close your eyes if you are comfortable and listen. Do you hear anything different with your eyes closed? Now pay attention to your sense of taste. What do you taste in your mouth right now? If you do not taste anything, what does "nothing" taste like? Finally, pay attention to your sense of touch. What can you feel right now touching your hands? What do your clothes feel like against your body? What is your body touching? If you are sitting, what is the feel of the chair? If standing, how does the ground feel against your feet? Continue to notice your senses for a few minutes, then open your eyes or look up when you are finished.

EMOTIONS AND SENSATIONS

Sit quietly and take some deep breaths. Scan your body for sensations. What sensations are you feeling? Don't judge them, just notice them. If you feel tension, try to let it go with each breath you take. Notice any emotions that are present as you breathe. Again, don't judge them, just notice them and name them. Continue to breathe deeply. If there is an emotion you don't want to hang onto, imagine sending it out of your body bit by bit with each breath. Continue relaxing and breathing in calmness with each breath and exhaling any sensations, emotions, or thoughts you do not want.

MINDFUL THOUGHTS

Take a deep breath and relax. Notice your thoughts as they move through your brain. Just because you think something doesn't make it true or real. Thoughts can come and go. Some thoughts stick with you for a while, others come and go quickly. Notice some of the thoughts you are having right now. Stop and consider them for a moment. Are they positive or negative? Maybe they are judgments? A judgment is just an opinion. Don't focus on judgments. Take a moment to recognize it, but then return your attention to your breathing and let it pass. If you are not having any thoughts that come to focus, that is fine. Continue to relax and breathe slowly, just noticing what is happening without judgment. There is no right or wrong way to be mindful. If you find thoughts entering your mind that cause uncomfortable feelings of fear, anger, or anxiety, notice them but bring your focus back to the present and to your breathing. You can stop this exercise any time if it is uncomfortable. If you are okay with your thoughts, continue to take deep breaths and notice where your mind goes.

PROGRESSIVE MUSCLE RELAXATION

In this exercise, you apply muscle tension to a specific part of the body and then relax that muscle group. First, focus on the target muscle group, for example, your right hand. Next, take a slow, deep breath and squeeze the target muscle as hard as you can for about five seconds. It's important to feel the tension but not to hurt yourself. It is easy to accidentally tense other surrounding muscles but isolating muscle groups will get easier with practice. After five seconds, let the tightness flow out of tensed muscles. Exhale as you do this step. Allow the muscles to become loose and limp as tension flows out. Deliberately focus on the difference between the tension and relaxation. Remain in this relaxed state for about fifteen seconds and then move on to the next muscle group.

Move slowly through each of the following muscle groups starting with your feet and systematically moving up to your forehead. After completing all the muscle groups below, take some time to enjoy the deep state of relaxation.

- Foot
- Lower leg and foot
- Entire leg
- Hand
- Arm
- Stomach
- Chest
- Neck and shoulders
- Mouth
- Eyes
- Forehead

NOTES

[1] Biegel, G. M. (2016, June 20). *Mindfulness-Based Stress Reduction*. PESI seminar presented at King of Prussia, PA.

[2] Meiklejohn, J., Phillips, C., Freedman, M. L. et al. *Mindfulness* (2012). 3:291. https://doi.org/10.1007/s12671-012-0094-5, copyright © 2012 Springer Science+Business Media, LLC.

[3] Emmons, R. A. and McCullough, M. E. (2003). "Counting Blessings Versus Burdens: An Experiential Investigation of Gratitude and Subjective Well-Being in Daily Life". *Journal of Personality and Social Psychology*. Vol 84, No 2, 377-389, copyright © 2003 by the American Psychological Association, Inc.

[4] Browning, E.B. (n. d.) *AZQuotes.com*. Retrieved from http://www.azquotes.com/quote/673994

[5] Bloom, S. L. (1997 and 2013). *Creating Sanctuary: Toward the Evolution of Sane Societies*. New York, NY: Routledge, copyright © 1997 by Routledge.

[6] Woods, J. (1899). *Dictionary of Quotations*. London, NY: Frederick Warne & Co., Bartleby.com, 2012. Retrieved from www.bartleby.com/345/authors/140.html, copyright © 2012 by Bartleby.com.

[7] Foles, N. (2018, February 5). *Nick Foles Amazing Super Bowl Postgame Speech* (Video file). Retrieved from https://www.youtube.com/watch?v=0vrlW3YP_Bg

[8] Dweck, C. (2016). *Mindset: The New Psychology of Success*. New York: NY: Random House, p. 6, copyright © 2006, 2016 by Carol S. Dweck, Ph.D.

[9] Dweck, C. (2016). *Mindset: The New Psychology of Success*. New York: NY: Random House.

[10] Steinberg, L. (2014). *Age of Opportunity: Lessons from the New Science of Adolescence*. New York, New York: First Mariner Books, p.24, copyright © 2014 by Lawrence Steinberg.

[11] Information on brain plasticity through various stages is based on a compilation of the work and research of Bruce D. Perry and the ChildTrauma Academy. A specific resource is Perry, B. D. (2013, September 6). The ChildTrauma Academy Channel. *SevenSlideSeries: The Human Brain* (Video file). Retrieved from https://www.youtube.com/watch?v=uOsgDkeH52o

[12] Debelius, D. (n. d.). *Adverse Experiences (ACES) Quiz*. Retrieved from https://www.safelaunch.org/aces-quiz/, copyright © 2018 by SafeLaunch.

[13] Felitti, V. J., Anda, R. F., Nordenberg, D., Williamson, D. F., Spitz, A. M., Edwards, V., ... Marks, J. S. (1998). "Relationship of childhood abuse and household dysfunction to many of the leading causes of death in adults: The adverse childhood experiences (ACE) study". *American Journal of Preventive Medicine*, *14*(4), 245-258. DOI: 10.1016/S0749-3797(98)00017-8, copyright © 1998 by American Journal of Preventive Medicine.

[14] Perry, B. D. (2009). "Examining Child Maltreatment Through a Neurodevelopmental Lens: Clinical Applications of the Neurosequential Model of Therapeutics". *Journal of Loss and Trauma*, 14:240-255, copyright © 2009 by Taylor & Francis Group, LLC. And Perry, B. D. and Szalavitz, M. (2017). *The Boy Who Was Raised as a Dog: And Other Stories from a Child Psychiatrist's Notebook*. New York, NY: Basic Books, pp. 327-330, copyright ©2006, 2017 by Bruce Perry and Maria Szalavitz.

[15] Starecheski, L. (2015, March 2). *Take the ACE Quiz- And Learn What It Does and Doesn't Mean*. Retrieved from https://www.npr.org/sections/health-shots/2015/03/02/387007941/take-the-ace-quiz-and-learn-what-it-does-and-doesnt-mean

[16] This chapter as well as those that follow are adapted with permission from the Neurosequential Model of Therapeutics (NMT) and the Neurosequential Model of Education (NME) developed by the ChildTrauma Academy. This information is a compilation of things learned while completing the requirements for NMT and NME certification. Specific resources for Chapters 10 and 11 include The ChildTrauma Academy Channel. (2013, December 31). *SevenSlideSeries: The Threat Response Patterns* (Video file). Retrieved from https://www.youtube.com/watch?v=sr-OXkk3i8E and The ChildTrauma Academy Channel. (2014, February 14). *SevenSlideSeries: State-Dependent Functioning* (Video file). Retrieved from https://www.youtube.com/watch?v=1uCn7VX6BPQ

[17] Perry, B. D. (1999). *Memories of Fear: How the Brain Stores and Retrieves Physiologic States, Feelings, Behaviors and Thoughts from Traumatic Events*. ChildTrauma Academy version. Retrieved from https://childtrauma.org/wpcontent/uploads/2014/12/Memories_of_Fear_Perry.pdf.

[18] Doidge, N. (2007). *The Brain That Changes Itself: Stories of Personal Triumph from the Frontiers of Brain Science*. New York, NY: Penguin Books, p. 252, copyright © 2007 by Norman Doidge.

[19] Eanes, R. (2015). *The Newbie's Guide to Positive Parenting: 2nd Edition*. N. Charleston, SC: CreateSpace Independent Publishing Platform, p. 40, copyright © 2015 by Rebecca Eanes.

[20] Perry, B. D. (2001, November). "Self-Regulation: The Second Core Strength". *Early Childhood Today, Volume 16, Issue 3*, p.20.

[21] Perry, B. D. and Szalavitz, M. (2017). *The Boy Who Was Raised as a Dog: And Other Stories from a Child Psychiatrist's Notebook*. New York, NY: Basic Books, p. xxviii, copyright © 2006, 2017 by Bruce Perry and Maria Szalavitz.

[22] Perry, B. D. and Szalavitz, M. (2017). *The Boy Who Was Raised as a Dog: And Other Stories from a Child Psychiatrist's Notebook*. New York, NY: Basic Books, p. 328.

[23] Harris, N. B. (2018). *The Deepest Well: Healing the Long-Term Effects of Childhood Adversity*. New York, NY: Houghton Mifflin Harcourt, p. 218, copyright © 2018 by Nadine Burke Harris.

[24] Perry, B. D. (2014). Neurosequential Inaugural Model Symposium. I first heard Dr. Perry speak about "Regulate, Relate, Reason" at the Symposium in Banff, Canada, June, 2014. Information can also be found in Perry, B. D. and Szalavitz, M. (2017). *The Boy Who Was Raised as a Dog: And Other Stories from a Child Psychiatrist's Notebook*. New York, NY: Basic Books, pp. 303-304.

[25] Van der Kolk, B. (2013, July 11). *Restoring the Body: Yoga, EMDR, and Treating Trauma*. OnBeing. (K. Tippett, Interviewer) (Audio file). Retrieved from https://onbeing.org/programs/bessel-van-der-kolk-restoring-body-yoga-emdr-treating-trauma/

[26] James, B. (1989). *Treating Traumatized Children: New Insights and Creative Interventions*. New York, NY: The Free Press, p. 1, copyright © 1989 by The Free Press.

[27] Wagenhals, L. D. and Lakeside. (2018). *Enhancing Trauma Awareness Training*. North Wales, PA: Lakeside, copyright ©2018 by L. Diane Wagenhals and Lakeside.

[28] Hiebert, M., Platt, J., Schpok, K. & Whitesel, J. (2013). *Doodles, Dances and Ditties: A Trauma-Informed Somatosensory Handbook*. Denver, CO: Mount Saint Vincent Home, copyright © 2013 by Mount Saint Vincent Home.

[29] Altman, D. (2014). *The Mindfulness Toolbox*. Eau Claire, WI: Pesi Publishing and Media, pp.29-33. Used with permission, copyright © 2013 by Donald Altman, M.A., LPC.

[30] Adapted from Hiebert, M., Platt, J., Schpok, K. & Whitesel, J. (2013). *Doodles, Dances and Ditties: A Trauma-Informed Somatosensory Handbook*. Denver, CO: Mount Saint Vincent Home.

[31] Adapted from Hiebert, M., Platt, J., Schpok, K. & Whitesel, J. (2013). *Doodles, Dances and Ditties: A Trauma-Informed Somatosensory Handbook*. Denver, CO: Mount Saint Vincent Home.

[32] Adapted from Dennison, P. E. and Dennison, G. E. (1994). *Brain Gym®: Teachers Edition, Revised*. Ventura, CA: Edu-Kinesthetics Inc., copyright ©1989, 1994 and 2010 by Paul E Dennison and Gail E. Dennison. Brain Gym® is a registered trademark of the Educational Kinesiology Foundation in Santa Barbara, CA. For more information about the Brain Gym program visit www.braingym.org.

[33] Dennison, P. E. and Dennison, G. E. (1994). *Brain Gym®, Teachers Edition, Revised*. Ventura, CA: Edu-Kinesthetics Inc. Brain Gym® is a registered trademark of the Educational Kinesiology Foundation in Santa Barbara, CA.

HEARTRATECHART   A

DATE	HEART RATE BEFORE ACTIVITY	HEART RATE AFTER ACTIVITY	COMMENTS

HEART RATE CHART

DATE	HEART RATE BEFORE ACTIVITY	HEART RATE AFTER ACTIVITY	COMMENTS